Simple Serenity

FIVE-MINUTE MEDITATIONS FOR EVERYDAY LIFE

Josie Robinson

SIMPLE SERENITY

ISBN: 978-1-954108-13-4

Printed in the United States of America
Cover and Interior Design by Jasmine Hromjak

EVERGREEN AUTHORS

First Printing: 2022
22 21 20 19 18   6 5 4 3 2 1

For mom, my meditation teacher.

"Meditation will not carry you to another world. It will reveal the most profound and awesome dimensions of the world in which you already live."

-ZEN MASTER HSING YUN

TABLE OF CONTENTS

How Five Minutes of Meditation Changed My Life

WHEN I WAS LITTLE, I used to sneak into my mom's bedroom each morning and watch her as she perched on the floor to meditate in lotus pose. She later told me that as soon as she sat down to practice, she would hear the door quietly open behind her, and a little three-year-old would sit next to her and mimic everything she did. When she chanted, "Om," I chanted, "Om." When she practiced pranic breathing, I did too. I don't remember any of this of course, but I appreciate that she let me sit with her.

As I got older, I stopped joining my mom each morning and preferred to do what kids did instead, but my mom continued her practice. It evolved and changed over the years—she added time for journaling and studying scriptures—but the thing that stayed the same was that she always took time to sit in silence. I admired her devotion but honestly thought it was something I would never do as an adult, mainly because I couldn't sit still for more than a minute. Also, the thought of "being" with my thoughts was a bit terrifying.

My mind had always moved a mile a minute, and meditation always felt impossible for me. I tried several times throughout adulthood to start my own practice. I read books, visited meditation centers, and took classes, but I couldn't get into it. I eventually gave up and resigned myself to the fact that I just wasn't cut out for it. My mom was the meditator, not me. I was much too high-strung.

But that all changed when my mom got sick.

On a crisp fall day that will forever be etched into my mind, my father called to tell me that Mom had been diagnosed with Alzheimer's, and the doctors said it was progressing quickly. Sometimes doctors are wrong about things, but unfortunately, that time, they were right and it was brutal. I watched my mom disappear before my eyes and be replaced with someone I didn't recognize. Our family provided her with the best care and support we could while she lived with this devastating disease, but it eventually took her life, and she passed away while in hospice.

I suspected something was wrong long before my mom received her diagnosis because she'd quit her morning meditation practice. Whenever I pressed her about why she'd given it up, she wouldn't give me a straight answer. Looking back on all of it now, I understand why she did what she did, but at the time, I was perplexed because her morning meditation was something she'd done as long as I could remember.

Around the time my mom quit her meditation practice was when I started my own, mostly because watching her fade away before my eyes filled me with overwhelming grief and anxiety that I didn't know how to cope with. I'd never been great at dealing with strong emotions, and the situation with my mom triggered me in a way I'd never experienced before. I needed something to help me calm down and deal with everything I was feeling, so I turned to meditation.

I started with just five minutes a day because I had read somewhere that's the minimum amount of time you need to experience the stress-relieving benefits of a meditation practice, and because that's all the time I had to spare. My life was full as a wife, mother, and business owner, and I knew if I were to add meditation to my daily routine, it had to be quick and easy.

So each morning, I set a timer for five minutes, closed the door of my office, sat on a pillow on the floor in a semi-crossed-legged position because I'm not that flexible, and focused on my breath. Every time a thought popped into my mind, I would say to myself, I take this thought in kindness and try to let it go because that's what I learned to do at a meditation center years ago.

Not going to lie, it was hard at first.

Five minutes seemed to stretch on forever, and I found myself constantly glancing at the timer to see if I was close to being done. It seemed like I was repeating that kindness phrase over and over because my mind was filled with endless chatter. Buddhists refer to this state as Monkey Mind, where the brain is unsettled and restless. I would say that is a completely accurate description of what was happening in my head when I first started a meditation practice. My mind was all over the place, swinging from vine to vine, going everywhere and nowhere all at once.

This went on for quite some time before I discovered guided meditations.

I read in one of my meditation books that to get your mind into a state of relaxation, you needed something to focus your attention on, like a mantra, your breath, or external objects like a candle flame or flower. Since trying to "empty" my mind obviously wasn't working, I decided to try this strategy instead and started focusing on something specific during my meditations. I turned to guided meditations I found online to learn how to do this. When I started practicing meditation this way, that's when everything changed for me and I finally realized what all the fuss was about.

From spending just a few minutes each morning in guided

meditation, my anxiety levels began to drop significantly, and I started to feel more calm throughout the day. My sleep also improved, as my mind seemed quieter at night than it usually was, and I fell asleep quicker and woke up more rested. For those tough nights when I had a hard day and couldn't stop thinking about what happened, I used guided sleep meditations and found that they calmed my mind so I could drift off easily.

But the biggest benefit was that meditation helped me get through an extremely difficult time of my life. For any of you who have ever watched someone you love go through the end of life, especially in a painful and tragic way, my heart goes out to you. It's an experience that gets imprinted onto your soul forever.

There were times as I watched my mother pass away before my eyes that I felt so helpless and hopeless that I thought I might be losing my own mind, as surely as my mother was losing hers. For those dark times, using guided meditations in the morning and throughout a particularly challenging day helped me reset, recharge, and remind myself that I was OK.

Eventually, I started to add a few more things to my morning meditation, like reading and journaling, just like my mom used to do, and I also began to stretch my meditation time from five minutes to twenty minutes. By that time, my meditation practice had become second nature, like brushing my teeth each morning, and I felt off whenever I skipped a day, so I make sure I don't unless I'm traveling. Even then, I'll still try to find a quick five minutes in the morning because I've found my day always seems to go better when I do.

It's been over five years since I started consistently meditating, and I can honestly say it's one of the best habits I've added to my life. I look forward to it each morning and feel so much more calm and focused for the day ahead when I finish. I'll get into some more of the excellent benefits of meditation in the next chapter, but for now, I want to share my story so you can be assured that if I can do this, so can you.

Look, I'm no meditation guru, and I didn't study in an ashram or monastery. Most of what I know about meditation came from my mom (who actually studied with a real guru), a lot of online searches, and reading every meditation book I could get my hands on. There was also a lot of trial and error to find a meditation method that actually worked for me (i.e., ones that helped me calm the heck down).

Really, I'm just an ordinary woman who needed something to take the edge off of everyday life, and meditation did that for me. My hope is that it does the same for you.

I had a full-circle moment recently when my youngest son came into my office one morning while I was sitting in front of my meditation table, reading one of my devotionals. Both of my kids are really good about not interrupting while I'm meditating, but they know that when I'm reading or journaling, it's OK to do so. He sat down next to me and softly said, "Mom, can you teach me how to meditate?"

"Of course," I told him, getting a little misty-eyed at the familiarity of it all. "Here's how you do it," I started, and I walked him through the basics. He was an excellent little student, and I was amazed by how much he already seemed to know. I realized then that he had been watching me each morning, just like I'd been watching my mom all those years ago.

Inside this book, I will teach you the basics of meditation and how to start your own practice so you can experience the wonderful benefits it has to offer and potentially teach it to others if you're ever asked to, which often happens when you've been meditating regularly because people start to notice that something seems "different" about you, that you're more peaceful and serene. This has happened to me more times than I can count, and I'm always grateful for the people who point this out to me because I can be really impatient about things like, "Nothing is happening when I meditate. It's not working!" Even though it obviously is.

My biggest piece of meditation advice is to be open, give it a try, and see what happens. I think you'll be pleasantly surprised at the benefits once you commit to the practice.

PART I

How to Set Your Meditation Practice Up for Success

ONE OF THE MOST COMMON questions people ask me is, "How do I get started meditating?" Then, they usually follow it up with a bunch of other questions, like "What position should I sit in?" "Where do my hands go?" "How long should I meditate?" and "What is it supposed to feel like?"

I love these questions because I had many of the same ones when I first started. Over the years, as I've talked to regular meditators, taken classes, and read books, I've found answers to many of these questions, and I'll try my best to answer them here so you can be well equipped to start your own practice. I've purposefully kept my answers brief because I've found that people often get hung up on the details, and it keeps them from actually starting a meditation practice.

The most important thing is to start. You'll be amazed at the difference five minutes of meditation a day can make in your life!

How long should I meditate each day?

If you are brand new to meditation, I recommend starting with five minutes a day. Several studies have shown that just five minutes of meditation a day is enough to help reduce stress and anxiety, calm the mind, improve your mood, and boost brain function. There's no issue with any amount of time you spend meditating, whether it's one minute or one hour; the most important thing is that you start.

As you find time for meditation in your daily routine, you can explore extending the time if it feels right to do so. I started with five minutes a day, and it was difficult at first, but the longer I stuck with it, the more I found myself wanting to extend the time because I really began to enjoy it.

The key is consistency. It's better to practice five minutes each day rather than an hour once a month because even just a few minutes is enough to calm and clear your mind and center yourself for the day ahead. When you do it every day, even for a short time, it's also that much more likely to become a permanent habit and an essential part of your life.

What position should I meditate in?

Depending on how flexible you are, you can sit in any variation of the lotus position—quarter, half, or full. You can also sit cross-legged, with your hips elevated on a meditation cushion, pillow, or folded towel.

You can also choose to sit in a chair if this is easier on your body or if you'd like to practice while at work or traveling. To get into the right position, sit in your chair with a straight back and your feet planted on the floor. Make sure your head and neck are in line with your spine. You may place a pillow behind your lower back for added support if needed. Really, the most important thing is to choose a pose that's comfortable so you can focus on your meditation.

If you aren't sure what to do with your hands while in a seated position, you can rest them on your knees or place them in your lap. You can also put them into a mudra position, which is what I personally do because that's how I was taught at my local meditation center. A mudra is a symbolic hand gesture used for spiritual ceremony and to calm the mind for meditation.

The mudra I use is called Dhyana Mudra and is the most common and widely practiced hand position among meditators. It is performed by resting the right hand on top of the left with your palms facing up and the thumbs slightly lifted so the tips touch one another.

Dhyana Mudra is specifically used to deepen your concentration and guide you toward inner peace and tranquility. The right hand, representing enlightenment and higher states of consciousness, rests over the left hand, which represents maya, or illusion. This is believed to bring balance to the two sides of the brain as a means of quieting the mind.

You can also lie down if this is easiest on your body. There is conflicting advice in the meditation community about whether or not you should lie down, but I personally think that whatever feels most comfortable is what you should do. Also, I've found for myself that when I'm feeling a lot of stress and anxiety, lying down and using a guided relaxation meditation is the most effective way to calm down and release tension.

To do this, simply lie on your back with your arms resting comfortably alongside your body. Your feet should be hip-distance apart, and your toes can be turned out to the side. If this is uncomfortable, bend your knees and place your feet flat on the floor or put a pillow underneath your knees to elevate them.

How do I find time to do this? My life is super busy!

First, find a time of day that works best for you. Many people like to start each morning with meditation, while others prefer to meditate in the evening. The time of day you choose isn't as important as the consistency of your practice. Consistency is key when it comes to reaping the benefits of meditation. My advice is to aim for a "same place, same time" approach so your mind and body become conditioned to the practice and it becomes an essential part of your life.

Then, start with five minutes of meditation a day. Many people give up on new health habits because they go too hard too fast. For example, a person who has never run before may decide to take up running and go for a three-mile, full-out run their first time out. They'll most likely end up sore, exhausted, and over it because of how bad the experience was. If they, instead, started with a gentle, five-minute run and then built up from there, they would have great-ly increased their chances of succeeding and actually liking running.

The same is true of meditation; sitting for thirty minutes your first time can be excruciating and make you never want to meditate again. That's not what I want for you because the benefits of this practice are amazing if you stick with it.

So, start with five minutes, then add more time if you feel in-spired to. When I first started meditating, five minutes felt like forever. Now, I practice for at least twenty minutes a day, and I'm always surprised at how quickly it passes.

Another way to make meditation a daily habit is to set up a ded-icated meditation space in your home. Having a meditation space reminds you of your intention to make it a part of your life and can get you into a state of tranquility as soon as you enter it.

Please be aware that your space does not need to be anything su-per elaborate or require its own room. I personally have a corner of my office set up for my space. All I have is a little table that I found at a consignment shop and a Zafu pillow that I bought from Etsy (for years, I used the pillows from my living room couch and they worked just fine). I have a few special mementos on my table, along with my gratitude journal and whatever devotional or spiritual book I'm reading.

By starting with just five minutes a day, setting up a dedicated space, and doing your meditation at the same time, you will greatly increase your chances of sticking with the practice and turning it into a regular habit that becomes an integral part of your life.

What do I do during meditation?

The most simple way to meditate is to sit and focus on your breath. Bring your attention to where you notice the sensation of breath, be it your chest, nose, or belly. Use that as your anchor, so you can come back to the sensation of breathing in that specific part of your body every time your mind wanders.

When thoughts arise—and they will—it's easy to go into them and forget to focus on your breathing. Just gently return back to your breath and body anchor and continue. You might find that you have to intentionally return to your breath over and over again, but please know this is completely OK. Be gentle with yourself and say, "I take these thoughts in kindness" every time you need to refocus. When I first started, I found myself repeating that mantra constantly and returning to my breath every few seconds.

Because I had such a tough time focusing on my breath, I found it helpful to have something more specific to focus on, which is why I turned to guided meditations and why the majority of this book is filled with guided meditations you can use for your own practice.

What do I do when I'm done meditating?

The time after meditation can be compared to the time after you've finished exercising. Serious exercisers always take time for a cooldown period to bring their body into balance after a workout, and you should do the same after you're done with your meditation.

If you abruptly get up from sitting and rush into another unrelated activity, it'll be tougher to feel the sense of calm and peace you experienced during your meditation time throughout the rest of your day. There is never a better moment to engage in a spiritual practice than the time right after you meditate, which is why I strongly recommended "cooling down" with another simple activity, like journaling or prayer.

I personally do the same practices I saw my mom do when she finished meditating. She always took a few minutes afterward to pray, read a spiritual book or devotional, and write in her journal. I now do the same after I'm done meditating and have found these simple activities to greatly enhance my practice.

At the very least, if you don't have time for anything additional after your five minutes of meditation, a quick and simple "thank you" is always a great way to end your practice. Put your hands into a prayer position and say, "Thank you for this moment. Amen," and carry that feeling of peace and gratitude with you through the rest of your day

PART II

30 Amazing Guided Meditations You Can Do in Just Five Minutes a Day

IN THIS SECTION, I WILL share my favorite guided meditations that you can do anytime, day or night. You can choose to do
a new one each day or pick a few meditations and repeat them as
many times as you wish. Again, the most important thing is to start
and commit to five minutes of meditation a day, then extend the
time if you feel inspired.

I've adapted some of these meditations from longer ones I've
found over my many years of searching, and some I learned directly
from my mom. But the thing every single one of these meditations
has in common is that they are extremely powerful. I'm a "pack in
as much good stuff as you can in as little time as possible" type of
person, and each of these guided meditations will do exactly that.

Each meditation has its own script, and you can either read it silently and follow along or record yourself reading the script on your
phone and play it back. The latter is what I personally did. When
I discovered a meditation I liked online or in a book, I rewrote the
script so it was shorter because many of the guided meditations I
found were thirty minutes to one hour long, and I just didn't have
the time. My guess is that if you're reading this book, you don't
either, so I've made sure to tailor all of these meditations to fit into
the busiest schedules.

Feel free to use these guided meditation scripts whenever you
need to, in the way that works best for you, or you can use them to
lead a guided meditation for your family, friends, or coworkers. In
my former life as a school counselor, I led many anxious teenagers
through guided meditations to help them manage stress and give
them a tool they could use to calm themselves during class. They
always seemed to visibly relax as soon as I started reading my script.
If you have people in your life who need help managing their stress
and anxiety, these guided meditations are a great resource to share
with them.

There's only one rule when it comes to these guided meditations: don't practice while driving or operating machinery. The goal of meditation is to put you into a state of relaxation, but you might find yourself becoming so relaxed you drift off, which is perfectly OK if you're in an appropriate place to do so, but not at all if you're in a position where you could hurt yourself or someone else. So, be sure to find a quiet, safe place to meditate in peace.

Although I have been meditating for quite awhile now, I'm not a medical doctor, so the meditations in this book should not be used as a substitute for medical treatment. Please check with your doctor before embarking on any new program, even one as gentle as meditation.

My biggest hope is that you enjoy meditation so much that it becomes a regular part of your everyday life. A little goes a long way when it comes to this practice, and I truly wish you all the best as you embark on the most important journey you'll ever take: the journey within yourself.

Namaste.

Five-Minute Morning Meditations

Refreshing Morning Sunrise Meditation
to Fill Your Day with Positive Energy

Uplifting Morning Meditation
to Bless Your Day with
Joy, Peace, and Harmony

Refreshing Morning Sunrise Meditation
to Fill Your Day with Positive Energy

Many ancient cultures around the world have believed in the healing power of the sun. Sun gazing, or watching the sun as it begins to rise, has been said to revitalize the mind and restore the body into health and wholeness.

You can practice this meditation by sitting outside during sunrise and simply gazing at it as it rises, giving gratitude for the moment. Or you can visualize the sunrise in your mind to harness its healing energy, which is what we will do in this guided meditation.

─────── GUIDED MEDITATION SCRIPT ───────

Find a comfortable position to sit in and close your eyes.

Let your breath flow naturally and easily.

Let your mind wander to a beautiful place in nature that makes you feel calm and comfortable.

You could imagine yourself walking along a sandy beach or sitting in the clearing of a forest.

Feel your body relax as you enjoy being in this beautiful place in nature.

Now, visualize that it's dawn, and the sun is just starting to rise.

Everything around you starts to get lighter and lighter as the sun rises to start a new day.

Feel the warm, glowing, life-giving light of the sun fill your entire body, bathing it in light.

Take a few slow, deep breaths and enjoy this warm, healing energy that injects every cell with light.

Feel the sunlight recharge every cell of your body, leaving you feeling refreshed and restored.

Now, feel your heart center glowing with this pure and powerful sunlight.

Feel this beautiful energy heal your body at all levels of your being: physically, mentally, emotionally, and spiritually.

Know that this sunlight lives within you, and you can call on it whenever you wish.

Feel deep gratitude for the sun and the healing it has provided for you today.

Slowly open your eyes, wiggle your fingers and toes, and notice how refreshed and revitalized you feel for the day ahead.

Uplifting Morning Meditation
to Bless Your Day with Joy, Peace, and Harmony

Morning is my go-to time to meditate because I feel like it helps my day flow much better.

Think about those days when everything seems to go wrong: you spill coffee on yourself, get stuck in traffic, deal with crabby people, and so on. If you think back to how that day started, you'll probably realize you were feeling rushed and frantic from the moment you woke up, and that energy carried throughout the day. If, instead, you took a few minutes in the morning to breathe, meditate, and set your intention for a calm and peaceful day, you could potentially turn that frantic energy around to have a much more enjoyable day.

This simple morning meditation will help you set your day up to flow more peacefully. Try your best to carve out a few minutes in your busy morning, and see how much of a difference it makes.

——— GUIDED MEDITATION SCRIPT———

Find a comfortable position to sit in and close your eyes.

As you find your position, begin your morning meditation with a gentle smile.

Inhale in through your nose slowly, and exhale through your mouth, letting go of any stress and tension you may be holding in your muscles.

Relax your hands on your knees or lap with your palms facing the sky.

Imagine yourself walking barefoot in a beautiful place in nature.

You can create any environment you wish; it can be a forest, a park, a beach, any place that makes you feel peaceful and calm.

Stop for a moment in your nature walk and feel the earth beneath your feet.

Feel the touch of nature in the soles of your feet as you imagine roots growing out of them, connecting you deep to the core of the earth.

Now that you are grounded, set an intention for a positive and peaceful day.

Think of what kind of day you wish to have. Do you have work to do? Do you have a free day and want to give yourself some time to relax? No matter what it is, set an intention to have a beautiful day filled with love, peace, and harmony.

Now, imagine yourself going through your day with a sense of calmness and inner peace.

Allow yourself to leave your body and float outside of it as your spirit, looking at the world from a bird's-eye view. Visualize yourself having a wonderful day filled with happiness and harmony.

Feel at peace with yourself and your life. Breathe.

Mentally prepare yourself to have a blessed day by imagining yourself completing your tasks with an open, calm mindset.

Stay here as long as you wish, and when you feel ready to start your day, pull your roots from the earth back into your feet, and feel deep gratitude for your amazing life.

Slowly move your chin over your right shoulder, then over your left shoulder, then open your eyes.

You can return to your beautiful place in nature anytime throughout your day to connect with the peace inside of you.

Have a blessed, beautiful day filled with peace, joy, and love.

Five-Minute Evening Meditations

Calming Ocean Waves Countdown Meditation
for Deep and Restful Sleep

Daily Examen Nightly Prayer Meditation to Let Go
and Let God Take Care of All Your Worries

Full-Body Progressive Muscle Relaxation
Meditation to Release Tension
and Fall Asleep Easily

Calming Ocean Waves Countdown Meditation for Deep and Restful Sleep

Sometimes it can be difficult to shut our minds off and fall asleep at night, especially if we've had a tough day or if we're feeling stressed. On those nights when I just couldn't fall asleep, the following guided sleep meditations helped me calm down and relax so I could drift off easily.

This first guided meditation was especially soothing to me, and even now, when I visualize ocean waves and writing numbers in the sand, I start to feel really sleepy. My hope is that these calming guided meditations help you have a restful night's sleep too.

———— GUIDED MEDITATION SCRIPT————

Find a comfortable position to sleep in. Take a slow, deep breath in, then slowly breathe out. Feel your body relax and sink into the bed.

Take another slow, deep breath in, and as you exhale, feel all the tension leave your body. Return to your normal breathing.

Visualize yourself on a beautiful sandy beach. Feel the sun warm your body and listen to the gentle waves lap along the shore.

Being on this beach makes you feel so calm and relaxed.

Visualize now that you're holding a stick in your hand. Use it to draw the number ten in the sand. Go slowly and take your time. As you draw, you feel your body getting heavy and sleepy.

Once the number is drawn in the sand, visualize the waves coming in and washing it away, leaving a blank sand canvas. Each crash of the waves makes you feel more and more relaxed.

Take your stick and draw the number nine in the sand. If you find that your attention drifts to other thoughts, that's OK. Gently bring yourself back to drawing the number in the sand.

Once again, visualize the waves washing the number away, leaving you feeling calm and relaxed and pushing you closer and closer to sleep.

Now, take your stick and draw the number eight in the sand. Notice the way you move it through the wet sand, your body growing heavier with every stroke. With each number you draw, you find yourself getting more and more relaxed.

Visualize the waves washing it all away, taking your tension along with it. You feel so calm, relaxed, safe, and peaceful.

Take the stick and draw the number seven in the sand. Remember to breathe slowly and deeply as you do so.

Soon, you see the waves crash in again, washing everything away. Their mighty sounds guide you deeper into total relaxation and sleep.

Now, use your stick to draw the number six in the sand. With each number you draw, you feel heavier and sleepier. Watch the waves wash it all away. You're so calm and relaxed now.

Don't worry if your attention wanders; just gently guide your mind back to the seaside and your drawing stick. Now, draw the number five in the sand, focusing deeply on how everything moves in harmony.

Another wave comes to wash it away. With each crashing wave, you feel yourself drifting more and more to sleep.

Use your stick to draw the number four in the sand. Notice how heavy the stick feels as you drag it through the wet sand. It's almost as heavy as your sleepy body.

The waves come in once again to wash it away. You feel so sleepy.

With your stick, draw the number three in the sand. The waves crash on shore and give you another clean slate, as you begin to pleasantly drift off to sleep.

Draw the number two in the sand with your stick. You feel so tired, almost unable to stay awake.

The waves submerge your feet and ankles, leaving you with a fresh, new surface to draw on. Your body is one with the bed and you are ready to sleep now.

Taking your time as you drag the stick through it.

The waves come one more time to claim another number. You watch the waves lap onto the sand and allow yourself to drift off to a deep sleep.

Daily Examen Nightly Prayer Meditation to Let Go and Let God Take Care of All Your Worries

Practicing gratitude is one of the ways I calm my mind each night before bed. Reflecting on what I'm grateful for instead of my worries instantly unknots my tension and puts me into a peaceful frame of mind for sleep.

My favorite way to practice nightly gratitude is with an amazing prayer meditation created by Saint Ignatius Loyola over four hundred years ago called the Daily Examen. The Examen is an easy five-step process you can use at the end of the day to calm your mind and deepen your spiritual connection with the world around you.

————— GUIDED MEDITATION SCRIPT—————

Lie down comfortably in your bed. Take a deep, calming breath in, then slowly exhale, feeling your body relax with each passing second.

Step one of the Daily Examen is to become aware of God's presence.

Feel God with you now and ask to become more conscious of God's presence.

It may be helpful to repeat a Psalm, like "Be still and know that I am God," or any other prayer that connects you to a Higher Power.

Take a few slow, deep breaths, and feel the warm, loving embrace of God surround and protect you.

Step two of the Daily Examen is to look back on your day with gratitude.

Take a moment to review the past twenty-four hours and think about what you're thankful for.

Think of all the people and places you encountered and the things that happened that make you feel blessed.

Take a moment to give thanks to God for providing you with these blessings.

Feel deep gratitude fill your heart as you say, "Thank you God for all the ways you showed up in my life today."

Step three of the Daily Examen is to take an honest look at your day.

Again, review everything that happened in the past twenty-four hours. Take note of your interactions with others and your emotions.

We often rush through each day without pausing to reflect. Deeply and honestly reflecting on the past day can help us learn more about ourselves and improve our future actions.

When you reflect on your day, don't judge any of your emotions or actions; simply observe them.

Step four of the Daily Examen is to choose a part of the day that was particularly rough and pray about it.

From your review, you may have found that God is directing you to work on something, whether it's an emotion, a relationship, or some other unpleasant situation.

Call the situation or emotion into your mind's eye and pray about it.

Ask for God's guidance to resolve it.

Feel yourself let go of the situation, releasing it into God's care. You know it will be resolved in the most benevolent way possible.

Step five of the Daily Examen is to pray for tomorrow.

Ask God to guide you tomorrow and lead you to your highest purpose.

Send love and light to tomorrow and pray for wisdom and strength.

Feel deep gratitude, knowing God has already answered your prayer and tomorrow is already blessed.

Take some slow, deep breaths and know that all is well.

Full-Body Progressive Muscle Relaxation Meditation to Release Tension and Fall Asleep Easily

One of the ways your body responds to anxiety or stress is with muscle tension. Stiff necks, sore backs, and frequent throbbing headaches are all signs our bodies are holding onto extra stress and manifesting it within our bodies. Progressive muscle relaxation is a method that helps relieve this tension.

During this meditation, you will focus on one muscle at a time, squeezing and contracting it for about five seconds, then totally letting it go. Take care not to hurt yourself while tensing your muscles; you should never feel intense or shooting pain while completing this practice. The muscle tension should be focused yet gentle.

───── GUIDED MEDITATION SCRIPT─────

This session is best done when laying in your bed before you fall asleep.

Close your eyes and prepare for deep relaxation.

Begin by breathing in slowly and bringing your awareness to your toes and feet. Take a deep breath in and squeeze your toes and feet for a count of five.

1 . . . 2 . . . 3 . . . 4 . . . 5

Now exhale, and release the pressure from your toes and feet and let them completely relax.

Feel all the tension leave as you release your muscles.

Next, move up to your calves, and as you breathe in, point your toes and squeeze your calves for a count of five.

1 . . . 2 . . . 3 . . . 4 . . . 5

As you exhale, completely relax your calves and toes and release all the tension.

Move up to your thighs, and as you breathe in, squeeze them for a count of five.

1 ... 2 ... 3 ... 4 ... 5

As you exhale, relax your thighs completely and feel all the pressure release.

With the next inhale, move to your pelvic area and clench your entire pelvis and lower back for a count of five.

1 ... 2 ... 3 ... 4 ... 5

Exhale and relax your lower back and pelvis into the bed. Let it all go.

Move to your abdominal area on the next inhale and squeeze your core for a count of five.

1 ... 2 ... 3 ... 4 ... 5

Exhale and feel all the tension effortlessly pour out of your body.

Move to your chest area, breathe in deeply, and clench your chest for a count of five.

1 ... 2 ... 3 ... 4 ... 5

Exhale a slow, controlled breath and relax your body, feeling all the tension leave this area.

Move your focus to your shoulders and neck, and as you breathe in, squeeze this area for a count of five.

1 ... 2 ... 3 ... 4 ... 5

As you exhale, let all of the tension in this area melt away and relax deeply.

Move to your arms and hands and squeeze them into fists with your next inhale. Clench for a count of five.

1 . . . 2 . . . 3 . . . 4 . . . 5

Exhale and feel your arms and hands sink into the bed. Notice how your stress and tension leave your body through your fingers.

Move up to your jaw and as you breathe in, clench your jaw for a count of five.

1 . . . 2 . . . 3 . . . 4 . . . 5

Exhale slowly and deeply, and relax your neck and jaw, feeling how tranquil and ready for sleep you've become.

Move up to the rest of your face, and as you breathe in, squeeze for a count of five.

1 . . . 2 . . . 3 . . . 4 . . . 5

Exhale and allow your head to melt into your pillow as you feel your stress leave completely.

Now, on your next inhale, squeeze your entire body, from your toes to your head, and hold for a count of five.

1 . . . 2 . . . 3 . . . 4 . . . 5

Exhale deeply and feel your body completely relax and melt into the bed. All the remaining tension comes out through your fingers and toes.

Five-Minute Guided Breathing Meditations

4-7-8 Pranayama Breathing Meditation to Replenish Oxygen and Create Instant Tranquility

Alternate Nostril-Breathing Meditation to Bring Your Mind and Body into Balance

4-7-8 Pranayama Breathing Meditation
to Replenish Oxygen and Create Instant Tranquility

This breathing method is based on the Pranayama yoga practice of controlling the breath, which involves holding the breath for a period of time, allowing your body to replenish its oxygen.

The breath technique known as the 4-7-8 method, created by Dr. Andrew Weil, can give your entire body a much-needed oxygen boost to promote healing. Dr. Weil calls the 4-7-8 method a "natural tranquilizer" for the nervous system. You can use this guided breathing meditation anytime you need a boost or need to calm your nervous system.

Please note that these guided breathing meditations may cause lightheadedness, so for anyone with a medical condition where this could be an issue, please talk with your doctor before using any of the guided breathing meditations in this section.

———— GUIDED MEDITATION SCRIPT ————

Start by sitting in a comfortable position, making sure your spine is straight to allow your breath to flow as freely as possible.

Gently place your tongue at the roof of your mouth and hold it there throughout the meditation.

Breathe in, then exhale slowly and completely with your mouth open, blowing the air around your tongue with a whooshing sound.

With your next inhale, close your lips together and breathe in deeply through the nose for a count of four.

1 . . . 2 . . . 3 . . . 4

Hold your breath, without straining, for a count of seven.

1 . . . 2 . . . 3 . . . 4 . . . 5 . . . 6 . . . 7

Exhale through your mouth while making a whooshing sound for a count of eight.

1 . . . 2 . . . 3 . . . 4 . . . 5 . . . 6 . . . 7 . . . 8

You have now completed your first cycle of breathing.

Complete this cycle two more times for a set of three.

To start, take a small breath in, then exhale completely with your mouth open, blowing air around your tongue with a whooshing sound.

Close your lips together, and inhale deeply through your nose for a count of four.

1 . . . 2 . . . 3 . . . 4

Gently hold your breath for a count of seven.

1 . . . 2 . . . 3 . . . 4 . . . 5 . . . 6 . . . 7

Exhale through your mouth, making a whooshing sound, for a count of eight.

1 . . . 2 . . 3 . . . 4 . . . 5 . . . 6 . . . 7 . . . 8

Repeat one more time.

Take a small inhale, then exhale completely out your mouth, blowing air around your tongue with a whooshing sound.

Close your lips together and inhale deeply through your nose for a count of four.

1 . . . 2 . . . 3 . . . 4 . . . 5

Hold your breath for a count of seven.

1 . . . 2 . . . 3 . . . 4 . . . 5 . . . 6 . . . 7

Exhale through your mouth, making a whooshing sound, for a count of eight.

1 . . . 2 . . . 3 . . . 4 . . . 5 . . . 6 . . . 7 . . . 8

You can practice 4-7-8 breathing whenever you need to calm your mind and body.

Start with three cycles, then work up to eight if you wish to build up the breath and relaxation response in your body.

———————————————————————————

Alternate Nostril-Breathing Meditation to Bring Your Mind and Body into Balance

Throughout the course of each day, our breath has a natural cycle that alternates between the right and left nostril, and each nostril switches dominance every four hours. This nostril-breathing pattern mirrors the natural polarity of our brains and maintains its balance.

When we stimulate nostril breathing with meditation, we further assist our brain's natural balancing act, resulting in a greater sense of calm in our minds and bodies.

I remember my mom doing alternate nostril breathing the most. She said it helped relieve her anxiety, and I frequently saw her use it during times of stress, like being in large crowds or after a difficult day at work. I now use it when I'm feeling stressed, and it really does calm me.

——— GUIDED MEDITATION SCRIPT———

To begin, sit in a cross-legged position on the floor or in a chair.

Make sure your spine is straight to allow the breath to flow effortlessly.

Start by closing your left nostril with your thumb, and breathe in slowly through your right nostril for a count of ten.

1 ... 2 ... 3 ... 4 ... 5 ... 6 ... 7... 8 ... 9 ... 10

Now, close your right nostril with your index finger and hold your breath for a count of four.

1 ... 2 ... 3 ... 4

Release your left nostril and exhale for a count of ten, leaving your index finger on your right nostril.

1 . . . 2 . . . 3 . . . 4 . . . 5 . . . 6 . . . 7 . . . 8 . . . 9 . . . 10

At the end of the exhale, pause for a count of four.

1 . . . 2 . . . 3 . . . 4

Now, let's switch to the other side.

Breathe in through the left nostril for a count of ten.

1 . . . 2 . . . 3 . . . 4 . . . 5 . . . 6 . . . 7 . . . 8 . . . 9 . . . 10

Close the left nostril with your thumb and hold for a count of
    four.

1 . . . 2 . . . 3 . . . 4

Release your index finger and exhale through your right nostril
    for a count of ten, leaving your thumb on your left nostril.

1 . . . 2 . . . 3 . . . 4 . . . 5 . . . 6 . . . 7 . . . 8 . . . 9 . . . 10

Continue this rotation as many times as you wish and enjoy the
    balance that is restored to your mind and body.

Five-Minute Mindfulness Meditation

Gentle Mindfulness Meditation
to Find Peace in the Present Moment

Gentle Mindfulness Meditation to Find Peace in the Present Moment

Mindfulness is the ability to be fully present and completely aware of where we are and what we're doing in a particular moment. Mindfulness is a skill we all possess, but it's not something most of us practice every day, which is why most of us find we're not that great at it.

In a flurry of jobs, appointments, and social events, we spend a lot of our days in an unmindful state, letting our mind wander all over the place. Unfortunately, the places our mind usually wanders to aren't great and can cause us a lot of unnecessary stress.

Practicing just a few minutes of mindfulness meditation each day can serve as a powerful antidote to our wandering minds and can make it easier to go from reactive to calm and focused.

———— GUIDED MEDITATION SCRIPT————

Choose a comfortable position to sit in, and close your eyes.

Inhale slowly, then exhale completely through your nose.

Allow yourself to connect with the present moment, right here and now, and simply become aware of your normal breathing patterns.

Take a moment to gently scan your body.

Notice all of the sensations in your body, and allow them to be there without any judgment or attachment.

Continue to gently breathe in and out of your nose and focus on being in your body, just as it is.

Now, move to your mind and thoughts. What thoughts are floating around?

Observe these thoughts as they come and go, and accept them. There's no need to be attached to them or judge yourself.

Allow them to simply be there. Watch them as a gentle observer.

Come back to your breath, becoming aware of its natural rhythm. Feel the way the air fills your lungs.

Now, bring your attention to your emotions. What feelings are coming up for you?

As you acknowledge your emotions, accept them without judgment.

Breathe slowly and deeply, knowing you are whole and complete and your emotions are simply reactions to your thoughts.

Now, open your eyes and notice your physical environment. Is it warm or cold? What do you smell? What sounds do you hear?

Breathe and take in everything from the world around you.

Connect with the present moment, and gently return to just the sound of your breathing.

Feel free to stay in this state as long as you wish.

Five-Minute Meditations for Anxiety

Super Simple Breathing Meditation
to Relieve Stress, Anxiety, and Overwhelm

Soothing Sound Bath Meditation
to Calm the Chaos of the Outside World

Chakra-Toning Meditation
to Unlock the Incredible Healing
Power of Your Voice

Super Simple Breathing Meditation
to Relieve Stress, Anxiety, and Overwhelm

If you need a quick dose of "keep calm and carry on," this short and simple meditation will help. It works to relieve your stress before it takes over.

If you're not in a space to do the full meditation, you can still use the basic breathing and visualization from this practice anytime you need to relax and reset.

——————— GUIDED MEDITATION SCRIPT———————

Begin this practice by sitting or lying down in a place you feel safe and secure, and close your eyes.

Place your hands over your belly, breathe in slowly through your nose, and feel your belly expand.

Now, exhale slowly out of your mouth, feeling all the air leave your belly as your body starts to relax.

Take another deep breath in through your nose, feeling your belly expand with air.

This time, on the exhale, let the air out in a big, audible sigh. Ahhhh.

Breathe in deeply through your nose and feel the air expand in your belly like a balloon.

Exhale and breathe out through your mouth, making a loud sigh. Ahhhh.

Visualize yourself letting all of your stress go with your out breath.

Breathe in again, and this time, visualize a beautiful, pearl-white light coming into your body as you breathe, filling your entire body with warm healing light.

Now, exhale and loudly sigh, seeing all your anxiety, worries about the future, and stress leave your body.

Breathe in the beautiful, white healing light that embraces you with love and healing.

Breathe out with a loud sigh, and let everything go, feeling so calm and peaceful.

Stay here in this state and relax, breathing in and out as long as you need to.

Let your entire being enter into a deep state of inner peace and stillness.

End this practice with a smile, knowing that all is well in this moment.

Open your eyes, wiggle your toes and fingers, feel a new sense of calm and peace, and carry that feeling with you as you move through the rest of your day.

Soothing Sound Bath Meditation
to Calm the Chaos of the Outside World

Pythagoras, one of the most influential philosophers in history, said sound, especially music, is one of the most powerful forms of healing available to us. Unfortunately, our modern world is filled with inharmonious sounds that knock us out of balance. Electrical hums, sirens, beeping appliances—all these things keep us out of tune. The best way to get back into tune is by taking a sound bath.

Researchers have found that daily applications of healthy sounds can lower anxiety and blood pressure, massage your internal organs, help release trauma in our tissues, release endorphins, and aid in cell repair. This simple sound bath meditation will help bring your body back into tune and restore balance and harmony.

———— GUIDED MEDITATION SCRIPT————

Before you begin this meditation, find your favorite sound to play, be it meditation music, dolphin and whale sounds, or any other sounds you find pleasing to your ears.

If you are able, place speakers by your head and your feet. If you only have one source of sound, place it at the top of your head with the speakers facing your body so the sound washes over you.

The most important thing is to find music you enjoy because that will provide the most effective healing from your sound bath.

Lie down in a comfortable position with your head and feet supported.

Allow the music to wash over you, cleansing away all your stress and the noise pollution of the outside world your body may have absorbed.

Let it all go.

Take a deep breath in through your nose, and exhale out your mouth, visualizing these healing sounds helping your body release all your tension.

Take another deep breath in, then exhale slowly, taking a moment to scan your body and notice any areas that feel pain or energy blocks.

You can relieve this tension by visualizing a golden river of light washing over this painful area.

Breathe normally and imagine this golden river of light running through the areas of your body that need healing. The river washes everything away in time with the music.

Visualize how each individual sound of your recording resonates with different parts of your body.

See this sound healing revitalize these areas of your body.

If you feel inspired, hum or sing along with the sound to release your tensions and drift deeper into healing.

Take another deep breath in, then exhale, visualizing your whole body being bathed in golden healing light and sound.

Enjoy this peaceful feeling for a few moments.

Now, let's go even deeper into our sound bath.

Stay immersed in the music and allow your mind to create a beautiful place.

This can be any beautiful place of your making, be it in nature, your home, or the stars.

Allow the music to guide you as you experience this beautiful place with all five of your senses.

Notice the sights, smells, and textures.

Completely immerse yourself in this glorious, sound-filled world.

Feel yourself in perfect peace and harmony as you listen to the sound and enwrap yourself in this beautiful space.

Feel free to bathe in your sound bath as long as you wish.

When you're ready, wiggle your toes and fingers and open your eyes.

Feel gratitude for being able to take a moment to heal your body today.

Whenever you need to, you can call on the feeling of peace by listening to your music or visualizing the beautiful space you created in your mind.

———————————————————————————

Chakra-Toning Meditation to Unlock the Incredible Healing Power of Your Voice

For centuries, many sacred spiritual traditions have utilized the healing power of vocal sound. One powerful way to unlock this sound healing power is by toning. Toning uses the vibration of your voice to bring your body into balance and harmony.

Toning works by way of the vagus nerve, which is the nerve responsible for creating a sense of relaxation in your mind. The vagus nerve is located next to your vocal chords, so toning with your voice stimulates this nerve and causes the body to calm and relax. Think of toning as your body's reset button, one you can push anytime you need to.

In this meditation, you will learn how to use vocal toning to balance your chakras, the main energy centers within your body, to deepen the healing power of sound even further and create inner tranquility.

———— GUIDED MEDITATION SCRIPT ————

Find a comfortable place to sit, keeping your spine straight to allow the energy to flow freely through your body. Close your eyes.

Bring your attention to the base of your spine in your root chakra. Visualize it glowing a bright, beautiful red.

Take a deep breath in, and on the exhale, make an "UHH" sound, like in "cup."

Allow your voice to flow with the sound, and hold it as long as it feels comfortable.

Repeat this on the next inhale. Deep breath in, exhale "UHH." Feel every muscle relax.

When you're ready, bring your attention a couple inches below your navel, where your sacral chakra is located. Visualize its intense orange color.

Take a deep breath in, and on your next exhale, make an "OOH" sound, like in "you."

Take another deep breath in, then exhale "OOH." Feel the vibrations of your voice and the brilliance of the color heal and harmonize your body.

Focus on the area right above your navel, where your solar plexus chakra is. Visualize its bright yellow color.

Take a deep breath in, and on the exhale, make an "OH" sound, as in "go."

Again, breathe in deeply, then exhale "OH." Peace and relaxation are settling in your mind and body.

Move your focus to the center of your chest, where your heart chakra is located. Visualize its vibrant, beautiful green color.

Take a deep breath in, and on the exhale, make an "AH" sound, as in "ma."

Take another deep breath in, then exhale "AH." Feel your heart chakra fill with love, peace, and harmony.

Now, focus on your throat and neck, where the throat chakra is located. Visualize its bright blue color, the shade of the sky.

Inhale deeply, and on the exhale, make an "EYE" sound, as in "my."

Take another deep breath in, then exhale "EYE." Feel the beautiful blue healing energy flow through your throat.

Bring your attention to your third eye chakra, located in the middle of your eyebrows. Visualize its beautiful, deep indigo color.

Take a deep breath in, and on the exhale, make an "AYE" sound, as in "say."

Inhale again, then exhale "AYE." You're feeling so calm and peaceful.

Finally, bring your attention to the top of your head, where the crown chakra is located. Visualize a bright, glowing white light pulsing around your head.

Take a deep breath in, and on the exhale, make an "EEE" sound, as in "me."

Inhale deeply again, then exhale "EEE." Feel the beautiful white light and vocal sounds bring you total healing to your mind and body.

Feel free to sit in a space of silence and receptivity for as long as you need to.

If you ever need a quick way to calm down, tone the sound "AAH" in the heart, then "OOH" in the sacral to ground yourself back into your body.

Five-Minute Meditations for Stressful Situations

Spiritual Cord-Cutting Meditation to Unblock Your Heart and Free Yourself of Toxic Relationships

Hands-on Healing Meditation to Help Your Body Recover from Illness

White Light Protection Meditation to Clear Negativity

Spiritual Cord-Cutting Meditation to Unblock Your Heart and Free Yourself of Toxic Relationships

Sometimes we become energetically tied to another person or a situation within our lives, and we have to find a way to reclaim our energy and regain our sense of self. A spiritual cord-cutting meditation is the perfect way to do just that. When you know you're ready to release old pain, toxic thoughts, or negative patterns but they keep haunting your mind, this meditation can offer some emotional freedom and help you move on.

It's difficult to live as your highest self when a part of you is always giving energy to someone or something else. When you can finally let go completely and cut the energetic cord that binds you, you can also set the other person free to move on. This is the ultimate blessing to yourself and the other person.

——— GUIDED MEDITATION SCRIPT ———

Begin by sitting in a comfortable position and breathing naturally.

Let your thoughts and emotions come and go. Don't judge anything that comes up; just allow it to be.

Feel free to call in a Higher Power to hold your hand and guide you through this meditation.

Close your eyes, and see yourself being bathed in a beautiful, loving white light of protection and healing. You are safe and unconditionally loved in this light.

Now, think of the person or situation you want to let go of.

Imagine this person in their light body, sitting in front of you.

See yourself in your light body, knowing that both of you are protected and safe in this space together.

Imagine both of you sitting face-to-face on a beautiful white lotus flower, with a safe space between you.

Visualize a shimmery silver cord appearing from both of your belly buttons and flowing through the safe space between you to connect your light bodies together.

This is the etheric cord that connects both of you in this lifetime and any other lifetimes you may have experienced together.

Imagine a pair of golden scissors appearing in front of you and cutting the silvery cord that connects you to this person.

The cord cuts easily, and you watch as it begins to slowly return to your light body until it disappears back into your navel.

Now that the cord is cut, say the following words out loud: "I let you go in love, peace, and kindness."

Imagine the person in front of you slowly fading away into a giant bright white light until all that is left is a soft, loving light.

Imagine now that a shining silver infinity symbol has appeared in the light, acknowledging that the connection has been released.

Repeat the following words one more time: "I let you go in love, peace, and kindness."

Stay here on this beautiful lotus flower, becoming aware of any thoughts and feelings in your body now that the cord has been cut.

Simply allow these thoughts and feelings to be with you in love and compassion.

Now that you have released this toxic connection from your life, strong emotions may arise when you see or think about this person.

Know that this is normal and completely OK. When this
   happens, simply repeat the affirmation in your mind: "I let you
   go in love, peace, and kindness."

Take slow, deep breaths in and out and feel grateful for the
   experience of letting go what no longer serves you.

Begin to float on your lotus flower back to the present moment.

Open your eyes and return to your day filled with peace,
   gratitude, and forgiveness.

Hands-on Healing Meditation
to Help Your Body Recover from Illness

Many cultures around the world believe that a universal life energy runs through our bodies, connecting us to everything. This energy has been called many names, like prana, chi, etheric energy, and so on, but no matter the name given, it's believed this energy can be harnessed to heal the body.

One of the most common ways to harness this energy for healing is through the use of therapeutic touch with practices like Reiki or massage. Some people report dramatic results from using hands-on healing, while others simply appreciate the stress reduction that comes from sitting quietly and receiving a soothing touch.

This guided meditation provides a beautiful way to harness this universal healing energy anytime you need it. Everything you need is within your hands.

—————— GUIDED MEDITATION SCRIPT ——————

Find a comfortable place to sit or lie down, and allow yourself to relax deeply.

Close your eyes, smile, and tell yourself: "I am relaxing my entire body, from the crown of my head down to my toes."

Take a deep, slow breath in, then exhale, calming each cell of your body.

Let yourself drift into a deep state of relaxation and feel your body become light as a feather.

Visualize a giant light, bigger and brighter than the Sun.

This light represents the Source, the Creator, God, or any Higher Power you may believe in.

Stay in this space and imagine your heart radiating a golden light that represents your soul.

This light comes out from your chest, traveling up to your neck, forehead, then through the crown of your head, up to the Source.

Now you are deeply connected with the Source and can see the bright light spin above the crown of your head.

This light enters your head, expands down into your chest, arms, and hands, then down to your legs and feet, coming out through your toes.

This healing golden light is completely encompassing, surrounding your body and aura.

As you bathe in this beautiful golden light, gently rub your hands together until they become warm or you feel a current of energy in them.

Your entire being is now filled with a healing light you can use to improve your symptoms.

Slowly begin to move your hands from your feet up your entire body.

Touch your legs, hips, stomach, arms, neck, and head with your healing hands.

Move your hands over your body until you feel balance and harmony in your whole being.

If you feel some pain in your body, hold your hands over that area for a few minutes to energize and heal it.

Continue moving your hands over your body as long as you wish, healing your body from any pain or illness you may be experiencing.

When you feel ready to end this healing meditation, send gratitude to the Creator for your ability to heal yourself and thank them for your life and body. Now, you can travel back to the present moment.

End this meditation with a big smile as you wiggle your fingers and toes, then open your eyes.

Return to your day filled with peace and love and trust that you are able to heal yourself whenever you need to.

White Light Protection Meditation to Clear Negativity

There may be times when you need help clearing chaos and negative emotions from your day, whether it be from an argument with your partner, being stuck in traffic, or the negative noise of news and social media.

This simple yet powerful guided meditation can offer you protection and create an inner sanctuary you can return to anytime you need it.

─────── GUIDED MEDITATION SCRIPT───────

Begin this meditation by closing your eyes and breathing slowly in through your nose and out through your mouth.

Take another deep breath in through your nose and exhale out your mouth, allowing your body to calm and relax.

Check in with your body to see where you're experiencing tension.

Take a slow, deep breath in, and on the exhale, release all your tension and gently guide yourself into a deep state of relaxation and inner peace.

On the next inhale, imagine that a bright white light energy is entering your body, filling and surrounding it.

Now exhale, and visualize all your negativity and tension flow out through your toes with the breath.

Notice how your entire body becomes surrounded by this pure white light, which protects and heals you.

You are glowing, and this light is keeping you safe and secure.

Keep breathing in this beautiful loving light, and visualize all your stress and tension easily and effortlessly come out of your being and drift out of your external world.

You are relaxed and calm as the light expands and surrounds your entire being like a shield.

See this bright white light shield protect you from all the things that no longer serve your highest good.

This light is a magnet, drawing all the negativity, pain, and suffering from your being, and attracting only those things that serve your highest and best purpose in love and light.

You are attracting more light, positivity, and peace into your body with the power of this healing light.

The light expands more and more, and you feel so protected and safe, so full of peace.

Live in this present moment, enjoying this sensation of protection and healing.

Feel how your spiritual shield of protective light grows thicker and stronger as you continue to breathe in and out.

Acknowledge that this light is always with you, and you can call on it by breathing deeply and visualizing the protective light anytime you need it.

Stay here as long as you wish, inhaling more healing light and exhaling all the things that are no longer good for the evolution of your soul.

When you want to end this healing meditation, send out gratitude for this time, your breathing, and your life.

Be thankful for your unique body and your ability to heal and protect yourself with this beautiful white light.

Gently open your eyes, and continue your day filled with inner peace, trust, and love.

Five-Minute Meditations for Emotional Balance

Powerful Sedona Method Meditation
to Release Emotional Blockages

Healing Flame Meditation
to Clear Negative Thought Patterns

Transformative Ancestral Healing
Meditation to Repair the Root Cause
of Your Emotional Wounds

Powerful Sedona Method Meditation
to Release Emotional Blockages

The Sedona Method is a simple yet powerful tool you can use at any time to help you let go of any unwanted or suppressed emotions. Many of our mental and emotional issues stem from trying to suppress, fight with, or talk ourselves out of our emotions. To achieve emotional freedom, you must express and release them.

In this guided meditation, you will learn the basic questions that form the foundation of the Sedona Method. These questions will allow you to express and release your emotions in a safe space and discover a new way to be at peace.

———— GUIDED MEDITATION SCRIPT ————

Sit in a comfortable position and breathe naturally. Relax and calm your body.

Call to mind anything that's currently challenging you, be it a relationship, career, health issue, or any situation that is bothering you.

First, simply ask yourself, "What am I feeling right now?"

Take a few moments to notice what you're feeling. It makes no difference what it is.

What's most important is that you are honest with yourself.

Let the feeling come naturally. Breathe it in.

Next, ask yourself, "Can I welcome this feeling as best as I can?"

Again, it does not matter what your answer is; just allow it to come spontaneously, without any thought.

Next, ask yourself, "Can I let this feeling go?" "Yes" and "No" are both acceptable answers.

You may feel yourself releasing the feeling just by asking the question, even if the answer is "No."

Simply reflect on the answer and know that whatever you choose is OK.

Finally, ask yourself, "When can I let this feeling go?"

This question is an invitation for you to release whatever is emotionally blocking you.

You might find yourself letting go as soon as you ask this question.

Again, there is no right or wrong answer. Letting go is a decision you can make at any time.

If your answer is "a week from now" or "next year," then you've already acknowledged that you want to let go and that you actually can.

If the answer is "Now," you can release it now.

Take a moment to notice how you're feeling now.

Do you feel like you've let the feeling go? You may already feel a small change, a lightness.

If you feel you need to release more, repeat these four questions until you feel a release, no matter how big or small it may be.

The more you practice the Sedona Method questions, the better you will get at it.

Use this method whenever you need to, and notice what happens as you do.

The key to this method is to deeply understand that letting go or releasing is a decision you can make at any time.

These questions simply encourage you to make a decision to let go right now. You hold the power within you to choose to let go or not. The choice is always yours.

Healing Flame Meditation
to Clear Negative Thought Patterns

Fire has been a source of light, warmth, and protection since the beginning of time. The element of fire is capable of completely and quickly transforming something, including our thoughts and emotions.

Using fire as a tool for transformation during meditation is a powerful way to cleanse yourself of any stuck emotions or old thought patterns that are no longer serving you. In this meditation, you'll learn to let everything go into the flames and enhance your inner peace.

———— GUIDED MEDITATION SCRIPT————

Before beginning this meditation, take a moment to place a white candle on a table in front of you.

Light the candle and, for a few minutes, stare at the flame, taking gentle breaths and letting your thoughts and feelings come to the surface.

Take as much time as you need to simply notice the flame and your feelings.

Don't judge what comes up; just let it be.

Now, close your eyes and see the flame in your mind.

Ask that all your negative, stressful thoughts be consumed by this flame.

Visualize these thought forms burning one by one in the light of the fire, cleansing all your stress and negativity with it.

With every exhale, release anything that does not serve you and tries to hold you down.

As you do this exercise, peace and relaxation will flood over your whole body as you release the negativity and anxiety in your mind and body.

Let go of any guilt you may be holding in. There is nothing you can do to change the past.

You can set an intention to learn and grow from it, but you cannot change it, so release it and set yourself free.

Release any fears that may be holding you back.

Decide to step out with boldness and courage knowing that if something doesn't work out for you, it is OK; there are other options to try.

Remain focused as you find the path that is perfect for you.

Inhale peace and calm, and exhale to release the fear of rejection.

Not everyone will appreciate your unique gifts and talents, and that is OK.

This world needs you to be authentically you.

Your light is like no other, so shine brightly.

Take another deep breath in, allowing peace and calm to fill your lungs. Exhale and release the fear of the unknown.

There are many people who will never realize their goals and dreams because they suffer under the weight of the unknown.

Set an intention to step out into the world with boldness and enjoy the adventure that lies ahead.

The adventure of the unknown allows you to enjoy each day as it comes, without worrying about what might or might not work or the things you cannot control.

Your adventure awaits, so enjoy it.

As we bring this meditation to a close, take a deep breath in and feel the candle flame in front of you restore your inner light.

Feel the flame restore your hope and peace.

Feel the flame provide refreshment and rejuvenation for your soul.

Allow the flame to remind you of the many little things that make your life absolutely amazing. You feel your heart overflow with gratitude.

When you're finished, open your eyes and relish in this refreshing feeling, determined to walk with courage and boldness.

Transformative Ancestral Healing Meditation to Repair the Root Cause of Your Emotional Wounds

Each person has their own unique family lineage, and within this lineage, it's typical for the same patterns to pop up generation after generation. Some people experience more severe cases of trauma and abuse, while others exhibit more subtle aspects of the control, shame, and guilt that's carried from person to person.

The key to unlocking emotional freedom within is being aware of these repeating patterns and doing your part to heal and ultimately change them. In this powerful meditation, you will be guided to release the patterns that have bound you and your ancestors. When you do that, you will not only be blessing your ancestors, but you will also receive the blessings of your ancestors.

——— GUIDED MEDITATION SCRIPT ———

To begin this meditation, be sure you will not be disturbed and sit comfortably where you feel grounded and secure.

Close your eyes and become aware of your normal breathing patterns. Gently breathe in and out through your nose, feeling your body relax.

Check in with your body to see where you're experiencing tension, and with each exhale, let it all go.

Live in this moment, and let your body relax.

Now, imagine that you're walking into a magical forest filled with majestic trees, their branches high in the sky.

You feel the earth under your bare feet as the wind and sun touch your skin. The mesmerizing scent of this forest makes you feel so peaceful and secure.

Hear the birds sing and the wind move the leaves of the trees.

Find a spot in this forest, maybe under a tree or next to a gentle stream, and sit down on the soft forest floor.

Become aware of your root chakra, which is located at the base of your spine.

This energy center is all about security and stability.

As you inhale the healing energy of the forest, imagine this chakra shining a bright red light. Exhale all the blockages from this sacred energy center.

Visualize roots growing from your root chakra deep into Mother Earth's core.

Feel your roots connect with Her heart.

Watch Her loving energy travel from Her heart deep into your root chakra and up to your heart space.

You feel protected, loved, and safe here. All your worries are melting away.

In this beautiful, safe, and grounded space, you can connect with all your ancestors who came before you, stemming from your parents and line of your grandparents.

Stay here for a few moments with them, and send gratitude to them for your ability to share space with them in this life and present moment.

The energy of your ancestors created you, and now, you can express your love and gratitude to them for being alive in this moment.

Repeat the following words, either silently or out loud: "I love you. I honor you. Thank you for this existence!"

Take a moment to feel deep gratitude to all of them, thanking them for the gift of life.

In this place of complete and total love and protection, say to your ancestors either silently or out loud: "I let go of all negative belief systems, emotional blockages, and any negative karma within my ancestral line in love and kindness."

Feel all the negative patterns leave your body and be replaced with deep forgiveness from your heart, knowing that all the people in your family did the best they could in their life.

Let it all go, and walk into a new path in your life in love, kindness, and light.

Bring your roots back into your body, and carry this loving energy with you after the meditation.

Stay here as long as you wish, sending out gratitude for your experience in the calming forest.

Thank Mother Earth for helping you heal yourself and your ancestors.

Come out of this meditation slowly, gradually becoming more aware of your external surroundings.

Wiggle your toes and fingers, open your eyes, and continue your day filled with love, kindness, and forgiveness for all beings.

Five-Minute Meditations for Spiritual Development

Enlightening Guided Meditation
for Intuition and Clarity from Your Higher Self

Beautiful Chakra-Opening Meditation
for Beginners

Inspiring Guided Meditation
to Connect with Your
Guardian Angel

Enlightening Guided Meditation
for Intuition and Clarity from Your Higher Self

MEDITATION CAN BE USED TO access inner wisdom from your higher unconscious or a higher universal force often referred to as God, All That Is, or Source. The more you meditate, the more access you can gain to this higher octave of wisdom.

Connecting with this higher aspect of yourself when you feel stuck or at a crossroads can light your way forward. The right answer always lies within, and this simple meditation will help you connect with the part of you that always knows what the right answer is.

——— GUIDED MEDITATION SCRIPT———

To start this meditation, find a place in your home where no one can disturb you for the next few minutes.

Sit comfortably, and close your eyes. Breathe naturally in and out through your nose and feel your body relax.

When you're comfortable, visualize a white, brilliant light and know that this beautiful light of Divinity is protecting you during this meditation.

Place your hands in a prayer position in front of your heart center, and either out loud or in your head, set an intention to connect with your higher self for guidance.

Relax your hands on your thighs with your palms facing upward, and imagine yourself sitting on a magnificently bloomed lotus flower.

Feel yourself float toward the center of the Universe, toward a brilliant, white light of unconditional love and peace.

Stay in this moment and continue breathing gently, basking in this healing peaceful energy of light and love.

As you sit on the lotus flower, surrounded by the white light of love, imagine a bright, golden light emanating from the center of your heart space.

This golden light is shining where your soul resides, and you can connect with it anytime.

Take a moment to connect with your soul, your higher self, and listen to what it wants to share with you.

Take notice of any images, feelings, signs, or symbols that arise. These are all ways your soul communicates with you.

Notice what comes up, what your soul wishes to share with you right now.

Stay in this safe, loving place and ask anything you want to know. Listen to your inner voice give you an answer.

Gently breathe in and out and stay on this magical white lotus flower, floating in the infinite Universe.

Bring your focus to the area between your eyebrows and visualize a soft, violet light shining from this area.

This is the place where your intuition lights your path ahead.

Awaken your intuition and ask for any guidance you need.

You have all the answers you need inside of you because you are a soul living a human experience.

Stay here for a minute or two and listen to your inner voice and guidance.

Reflect every image, feeling, or symbol your intuition shares with you.

Stay here as long as you wish, asking for guidance and support in any area of your life.

Now, express your gratitude for your higher self; thank Them for sharing this guidance with you. You know you are never alone because there is always a loving Presence available to you whenever you need it.

Float on the lotus flower back to the present moment and become aware of your external world.

Open your eyes and smile.

Journal everything that came up during this meditation, and over the next few days, be on the lookout for messages from your soul throughout the day.

By regularly practicing this meditation, you'll open up to your higher guidance and wisdom and truly understand that you're never alone in this Universe.

Beautiful Chakra-Opening Meditation for Beginners

Adding mantras to your meditation can help balance the energies of your chakras and stimulate the endocrine system with the vibration of sound. Many ancient spiritual traditions believed that each and every part of our body functions at a specific rhythm, and if we tune into these rhythms by "singing their song," we can harmonize them.

A beautiful way to "sing" into our chakras is with Bija (pronounced "beej") Mantras. In Sanskrit, Bija translates to "seed." Think of this guided chakra meditation as water for the seeds of your soul, bringing your mind and body into balance.

———— GUIDED MEDITATION SCRIPT ————

Find a comfortable place to sit, keeping your spine straight to allow the energy to flow freely through the body, and close your eyes.

Bring your attention to the base of your spine at your root chakra and visualize it glowing a bright, rich, red color.

Take a deep breath in, and on the exhale, then slowly make the sound "LAM," with a deep "um."

Let it come out naturally; don't worry about how it sounds.

Hold the sound as long as it feels comfortable to do so.

Take another deep breath in, then exhale "LAM."

As you hold the sound, think of the affirmation "I am."

One more time, inhale deeply. Exhale "LAM." I am.

Now, focus on the area a couple inches below your navel, at your sacral chakra, and visualize a warm orange glow.

Take a deep breath in and, on the exhale, make the sound "VAM," with another deep "um."

Inhale, then exhale "VAM."

As you hold the sound, think of the affirmation "I feel."

One more time, inhale slowly and deeply, then exhale "VAM." I feel.

Now, focus on the area right above your navel, at your solar plexus chakra, and visualize a beautiful, bright yellow light.

Take a deep breath in, and on the exhale, make the sound "RAM," with a deep "um" vowel tone.

Inhale, then exhale "RAM."

As you hold the sound, think of the affirmation "I do."

One more time, inhale, then exhale "RAM." I do.

Bring your attention to the center of your chest, at your heart chakra, and visualize a beautiful glowing green orb.

Take a deep breath in, and on the exhale, make the sound "YAM," like "yum."

Again, deep breath in, then exhale "YAM."

As you hold the sound, think of the affirmation "I love."

One more time, inhale, then exhale "YAM." I love.

Bring your attention to the throat chakra and visualize a beautiful light blue glow.

Take a deep breath in, and on the exhale, make the sound "HAM," like "hum."

Again, deep breath in, then exhale "HAM."

As you hold the sound, think of the affirmation "I speak."

One more time, inhale, then exhale "HAM." I speak.

Focus your attention on the middle of your forehead, at your third eye chakra, and visualize a deep violet color.

Take a deep breath in, and on the exhale, make the sound "OM." Feel your chest vibrate from the sound.

Inhale, then exhale "OM."

As you hold the sound, think of the affirmation "I see."

Inhale one more time. Then, exhale "OM." I see.

Finally, bring your attention to the top of your head, at your crown chakra, and visualize a bright, glowing white light.

This time, silently say "OM" in your mind as an acknowledgement that you are receiving information and listening to your highest wisdom.

Breathe slowly and deeply, and chant "OM" in your mind.

Again, deep breath in, then chant "OM."

As you hold the sound in your mind, think of the affirmation "I understand."

One more time, chant "OM" as you breathe.

Feel free to sit in a space of silence and receptivity for as long as you need to.

When you're ready to finish the meditation, wiggle your fingers and toes to ground your energy and center yourself within your body.

Open your eyes and bring this new energy with you as you move through your day.

Inspiring Guided Meditation
to Connect with Your Guardian Angel

It is believed that an angel is placed by your side from the moment you are born until the moment you take your last breath. This angel is your ally through all seasons of life and can be called on for help, guidance, and support whenever you need them.

This meditation offers you a way to connect with your Guardian Angel during those times of need or if you feel ready to open the lines of communication with the angelic realm for love and support each day.

——————— GUIDED MEDITATION SCRIPT———————

Take a moment to get comfortable, and allow your breathing to find its natural pacing.

This will allow your mind to settle as well as send a signal to your muscles to relax.

As you continue to breathe normally, mentally scan your body to find and release any tense areas.

Close your eyes if they aren't already and gently roll your shoulders, stretching your chin all the way up, then down to your chest.

This is your time to step away from the demands of the day to extend kindness and compassion to yourself.

If your thoughts wander, bring your attention back to your body and breath.

Imagine a stunning, brilliant white light shining down from the sky.

Gently open your arms and reach for it. Feel yourself receive it.

You notice a light-filled form emerging in front of you, and you instinctively know this is your Guardian Angel.

In the presence of this light, you feel loved and cherished.

You feel peaceful and at complete ease, knowing deep within that you are safe with them.

Your angel beckons you to a beautiful crystal bridge.

Gaze at the bridge for a moment and pay attention to the way light interacts with its sparkling beauty.

Allow your hand to gently flow over the handrails as you slowly walk across this crystal bridge.

You can completely trust your angel.

Your Guardian Angel informs you that crossing the bridge will lead you to the realm of angels.

You willingly cross the bridge, with your Guardian Angel by your side. Everything is calm and serene.

Your angel leads you to a stone bench in the middle of a beautiful garden filled with blossoming trees, singing birds, and a musical stream.

You are completely at ease, feeling safe and peaceful.

Take a moment to tell your angel something that's been troubling you and ask for advice.

There is no need to hold back; your angel loves and supports you unconditionally and passes no judgment.

If you don't understand what your Guardian Angel is telling you, ask them to present the information in a different way.

Confide everything to them and let it all go to your angel to take care of. Take all the time you need.

When you feel that your time with your Guardian Angel has come to an end, thank them for being with you and for the information you've received.

Cross back over the crystal bridge and return to the present moment. Open your eyes.

Be on the lookout for any messages from your Guardian Angel in the days ahead.

Remember, your angel is always with you, and you can return for guidance and support whenever you need them.

———————————————————

Five-Minute Manifestation Meditations

Guided Golden Door Meditation
to Manifest Your Dreams into Reality

Heart-Opening Meditation
to Allow Abundance to
Flow to You Easily

Guided Golden Door Meditation
to Manifest Your Dreams into Reality

This meditation is based on a dream I had a few years ago during a time when I was frustrated and having trouble manifesting what I wanted. This dream revealed to me the way to manifest your desires into reality, be it love, abundance, health, happiness, or anything else: quit forcing things to happen, and instead, surrender and trust your Higher Power to bring what you need in the way that serves you best.

Once I started letting go and letting God, that's when solutions to my problems started showing up that were much better than anything I could have dreamed up myself.

─────── GUIDED MEDITATION SCRIPT ───────

Find a comfortable position to sit in, and close your eyes. Take a few slow, deep breaths to calm and relax your mind.

Visualize yourself standing in a peaceful void, a place where you can dream of anything your heart desires. What do you wish to create in your life right now?

Think of all the things you dream about, be it a new romantic relationship, more money and abundance, a new home or a fulfilling career, a deeper spiritual connection with the divine, the Earth being restored to her natural beauty, or anything else.

Take a few moments to simply reflect on what you most desire for yourself.

Now, imagine all those things you've wished for are being held for you in a grand, golden room.

Everything you've ever wished for is there, right now, in that beautiful golden room.

This golden room energizes your wishes and dreams and keeps them safe for you.

Now, visualize yourself standing in front of a golden door. This door leads to the grand room that holds all your dreams and wishes.

There is a small opening right at eye level that allows you to see into the room.

As you look through the opening, you see all your wishes and dreams in this beautiful golden room, being lovingly cared for and protected.

A light-filled being floats toward the door and opens it for you.

Allow this light being, this angel, your Higher Power, to effortlessly let you in.

You know deep down that everything in your golden room will be easily and effortlessly brought through the door for you in divine time for your highest and best purpose.

Let go of all your stress and tension around forcing the door open and bringing everything to you now.

Let go and let God. Breathe.

Let go of all your worries and have faith that everything from the golden room will come through the door when and if it's best for your highest purpose.

Now, allow the images of the golden door and room to fade from your mind.

Your wishes and dreams are in good hands and will be answered in divine time.

Open your eyes and give yourself a few moments to adjust back to the physical world.

As you go through the days ahead, be open to any signs that your dreams are manifesting.

Be aware these solutions may come completely unexpectedly, but they will ultimately be for your highest and best purpose.

If it feels easy and brings you joy, act on any blessings that come your way.

This is a signal from the divine that your wishes are being brought through.

As your dreams manifest, give deep gratitude for them coming true.

Heart-Opening Meditation
to Allow Abundance to Flow to You Easily

The root cause for many people's manifestation struggles is their difficulty to receive. These people typically excel at giving and are open-hearted and generous to everyone around them, but receiving is another story. They may feel like they don't deserve abundance and find ways to reject it if it comes their way.

Having struggled with receiving myself, I am intimately familiar with this issue and have found that the most helpful way to heal it is by addressing the root cause of my negative thought patterns around it. This heart-opening meditation has helped me allow myself to receive more love and abundance into my life, and I hope it can do the same for you.

——— GUIDED MEDITATION SCRIPT ———

Begin this practice by sitting in a comfortable position and closing your eyes.

Breathe deeply in and out, paying particular attention to how the air travels into your body and expands your chest and belly.

Relax your entire body, from your toes up to the crown of your head.

Feel your body calm as you focus on the natural rhythm of your breath.

If thoughts come, accept them without any judgment and simply return to your breath.

As you stay here, relaxed and peaceful, set an intention to let go of all the things that are no longer good for you and are not for your highest purpose in this life.

With every inhale, imagine that you're breathing in divine energy, and with each exhale, imagine you're breathing out all the negativity stored in your body.

Let go of all the limiting thoughts, patterns, belief systems, and emotional blockages living in your heart space. Watch them leave as easily as the breath leaves your body.

Allow all the beliefs of not being good enough or not being worthy to come to the surface right now. Sit with these beliefs without judgment; simply acknowledge that they exist.

Now, let them all go. Watch those outdated belief systems leave you easily and effortlessly.

Allow any and all emotions regarding guilt and shame around abundance to come to the surface now. Acknowledge how these emotions have hurt you.

Now, let them all go. Watch these negative emotional patterns of guilt and shame leave you now, easily and effortlessly.

Allow any feelings of lack, limitation, and not having enough from family or while growing up to come to the surface now. Take a few moments to sit with these feelings, without any judgment.

Let them all go. Watch all these feelings of lack and limitation, and of external negativity to leave you easily and effortlessly.

You feel lighter and peaceful in this moment as your body easily releases all these unnecessary thought patterns and emotions.

The words you say to yourself are powerful, so say the following affirmations out loud:

"I am worthy to receive all the abundance life has to offer me."

"I am worthy to receive all the abundance life has to offer me."

"I accept abundance with an open heart and mind."

"I accept abundance with an open heart and mind."

With each repetition of an affirmation, feel deep gratitude in your heart, knowing you have healed yourself at your core.

Abundance is on its way to you, and you are open to receive it in this loving space.

Envision yourself receiving many blessings, love, and fulfillment.

Imagine yourself receiving all the blessings you want, whether it's love, friends, money, or health.

Abundance and prosperity are not just about money; they are also about health, love, and happiness.

Watch how your life changes as you receive these blessings, how all the things you need come into your life effortlessly because you are now in a place to receive them.

Stay here as long as you need, and think about what you want to attract to your life.

Imagine these things coming in effortlessly.

The most powerful tool for manifestation is visualization, so imagine all the blessings and love coming into your life.

When you're ready to end this meditation, send out gratitude for the time you have taken for yourself and all the blessings that are on their way to you now.

Return to your day filled with trust, fulfillment, and faith that you are able to manifest anything you want into your life. Open your eyes and smile.

Five-Minute Self-Compassion Meditations

Healing Ho'oponopono Meditation
to Find Peace through Forgiveness

Simple Self-Love Meditation
to Nourish Your Heart and Soul

Grounding Tree of Life Meditation
to Connect With Your Inner Strength

Healing Ho'oponopono Meditation
to Find Peace through Forgiveness

Ho'oponopono is the ancient Hawaiian practice of forgiveness and one of the most powerful forms of self-healing available to us. The literal translation of Ho'oponopono is "to put to right; to put in order or shape, correct, revise, adjust, amend, regulate, arrange, rectify, tidy up, make orderly or neat."

In a nutshell, it means putting yourself back together, lovingly.

According to the ancient Hawaiians, error arises from our thoughts because we are holding onto painful memories from the past. When you recognize and heal the origin of those thoughts from a place of love and forgiveness, you heal yourself and everyone around you. You heal the world.

——— GUIDED MEDITATION SCRIPT———

Ho'oponopono is extremely simple, but extremely profound. All it requires is for you to repeat the following mantra:

"I love you. I'm sorry. Please forgive me. Thank you."

We will use this mantra to heal the core of your negative thought patterns to help you find compassion and emotional freedom.

Begin by sitting in a comfortable position and breathing naturally.

Let your thoughts and emotions come and go. Don't judge anything that comes up; just allow it to be.

Feel free to call in a Higher Power to assist you with this meditation, to hold your hand and guide you.

Imagine yourself bathed in a soft rose-gold light of protection and healing.

You are safe and loved in this light.

Now, visualize a relationship in your life that you are struggling with.

Imagine that person sitting in front of you and know that you are safe and protected in this light-filled space.

Place both hands over your heart, and gently say the person's name, silently or aloud, followed by, "I love you. I'm sorry. Please forgive me. Thank you."

Both of you are being bathed in the beautiful soft pink light. Again, say their name silently or aloud, followed by, "I love you. I'm sorry. Please forgive me. Thank you."

If any strong emotions come up, that's OK. Allow them to flow through you and release.

Repeat this process again, saying the person's name followed by, "I love you. I'm sorry. Please forgive me. Thank you."

Then, allow whatever needs to come to the surface to come. Feel yourself release and let go.

One more time, say the person's name followed by, "I love you. I'm sorry. Please forgive me. Thank you."

Now, let go of the image of the person and take a few moments to sit with your thoughts and feelings. Take a few easy, deep breaths.

You are deeply loved. You are safe and protected.

Feel the warm, soft rose-gold light embracing you. It is now time to turn this beautiful healing love and forgiveness toward yourself.

Imagine now that there is a mirror in front of you and you can see your reflection in this mirror.

Place your hands over your heart and watch the loving rose-gold light surround you and your reflection.

Say your name silently or aloud followed by, "I love you. I'm sorry. Please forgive me. Thank you."

Let any emotions come up that need to. Be gentle with yourself. It's OK to forgive yourself now.

You're being bathed in the soft rose-gold light. Again, say your name followed by, "I love you. I'm sorry. Please forgive me. Thank you."

It's OK. You are so loved. Breathe.

Again, repeat your name and say, "I love you. I'm sorry. Please forgive me. Thank you."

One more time, repeat your name and say, "I love you. I'm sorry. Please forgive me. Thank you."

When you are ready, let go of the images or thoughts.

Bring your awareness back to your body and take a few slow, deep breaths. Notice how you are feeling.

Offer gratitude to yourself for taking the time to heal your heart and take care of yourself.

Open your eyes, and return to the present moment.

You can repeat the Ho'oponopono mantra anytime throughout the day.

Love and peace be with you, always.

Simple Self-Love Meditation to Nourish Your Heart and Soul

Self-judgment and negative self-talk are unfortunately very common. A powerful antidote to this is practicing love and kindness to ourselves.

Research has shown that spending a few moments each day practicing a self-love meditation, such as the one below, not only makes you happier, more creative, and more energetic, but it also opens your heart to others. By taking care of yourself, you'll learn to live a happier life, which will inspire others to take note and start improving theirs as well.

 GUIDED MEDITATION SCRIPT

Find a comfortable position to sit or lie down. Begin by slowly and gently inhaling through the nose and out through the mouth.

Again, inhale through the nose and out through the mouth. Feel your body relax.

Now, place both hands over your heart and close your eyes.

In this relaxed state, become aware of your mind and body. Notice where your body is holding onto tension and what thoughts and feelings are coming up right now.

Don't pass any judgment on what comes up; just view it all as a compassionate observer.

No matter what you're thinking and feeling, no matter what comes up, it is OK to allow it to be there.

Continue to focus on your breath. On your next inhale, think, "I am worthy of love."

On the exhale, think, "I love who I am."

Again, inhale, "I am worthy of love."

Now, exhale, "I love who I am."

With each inhale, visualize yourself drawing in this healing self-love energy, and on the exhale, let go of everything that is no longer serving you.

Again, inhale, "I am worthy of love."

Now, exhale, "I love who I am."

One more time, "I am worthy of love."

And exhale, "I love who I am."

Let it all go now, easily and effortlessly.

Sit for a minute, and notice how you feel as you say these words to yourself. Whatever thoughts and feelings come up as you repeat your mantras are completely OK.

Now visualize the light body version of you standing in front of you.

This version is the highest part of yourself, your soul, filled with pure love and divine wisdom.

See this version of yourself clearly in front of you, smiling and sending you so much love and compassion.

Visualize yourself embracing this divine part of you, and feel the brilliant love and healing that comes from being close with this aspect of yourself.

Tell yourself, "I love you. Thank you."

This part of you is always with you, loving you at every moment. Imagine yourself merging with this divine love- and light-filled part of yourself and becoming one with its amazing energy.

Let this love permeate your entire being, filling your heart then your whole body.

Take a moment to enjoy this feeling. Love is always available for you whenever you need it.

When you're ready, take a few more deep, slow breaths, then softly open your eyes.

Sit for a few moments to acknowledge the powerful experience you had during this meditation, and appreciate the time you took to take care of yourself today.

Grounding Tree of Life Meditation
to Connect with Your Inner Strength

The Tree of Life is one of the oldest symbols and is commonly depicted as a large tree with roots that spread inward to the ground and branches that spread outward to the sky. This symbol represents us as human beings; just as the branches of a tree strengthen and grow upward to the sky, we too grow stronger as we move through life gaining new experiences and wisdom.

Calling on the Tree of Life in meditation is a beautiful way to ground and center your energy and deeply connect with the amazing healing power of nature.

──────── GUIDED MEDITATION SCRIPT────────

Find a comfortable, quiet place to sit, stand, or lie down for this meditation.

Start by taking a deep breath in through your nose and exhale out your mouth.

Feel your body relax as you inhale and exhale. Close your eyes.

Imagine you are transformed into a huge, magnificent tree.

Feel your roots grow deep into the Earth, grounding you.

Feel your strong, sturdy trunk and long branches reach high into the sky.

Now, take another slow breath in and picture the breath coming in through your roots, entering through the soles of your feet.

See your breath going up, up, up, high into the tree through your legs and chest, then to the top of your head.

Now, exhale through your mouth, blowing all the air out.

Again, take another deep inhale through your nose, pulling the air through your feet to the rest of your body. On the next exhale, picture all the leaves on the tree blowing away in the wind, just like they do every autumn.

As the leaves fall, so does all your stress and tension.

It falls away easily.

Take another long, slow, deep breath through your roots and up into your body, and exhale out your mouth, blowing all your stress and tension away with the leaves.

Continue to take a few more deep breaths in through your roots and out through your mouth, as the leaves easily fall away along with all your stress.

Continue to breathe until all the leaves and all your stress and tension are gone.

Enjoy the feeling of peace that comes from letting it all go and being a strong, healthy, magnificent tree.

Now, take another long inhale through your nose and your roots all the way up to the top of your body, and as you exhale, imagine that beautiful, bright, shimmering green leaves begin growing on the branches of your tree.

Inhale again through your roots, feeling your breath rejuvenate and heal you from the ground up.

Now exhale, blowing the air into your beautiful new growth.

With each inhale and exhale, picture your tree growing more and more beautiful, bright-green leaves and becoming stronger and more refreshed.

Keep breathing, and feel the sun shine on your beautiful new leaves, warming and healing your body all the way to your roots.

Enjoy the feeling of peace that comes from being a magnificent Tree of Life.

End your meditation by sending love and appreciation to the tree, saying thank you to the healing it has provided you. You can visit your tree anytime you need to.

When you're ready, allow yourself to transform back to your body and bring the feeling of peace back with you.

Open your eyes, wiggle your toes and fingers, and give yourself a few moments to adjust.

Feel free to visualize this magnificent tree in your mind whenever you wish to connect with the strength and serenity it provides.

Five-Minute Gratitude Meditations

Guided Gratitude Meditation to
Count Your Blessings and Brighten Your Outlook

Full-Body Gratitude Meditation to Tame
Negative Self-Talk
and Love Yourself Just As You Are

Soulful Gratitude in Advance Meditation
to Bring Your Best Life into Being

Guided Gratitude Meditation
to Count Your Blessings and Brighten Your Outlook

A wealth of research has been done on the benefits of gratitude—and for good reason. Time and again, studies show that practicing gratitude has a huge impact on overall happiness, positivity, and emotional resilience. On a personal note, practicing gratitude completely transformed my life for the better, so much so that I wrote two books about my experiences.

As a way to bring about the best of both worlds of gratitude and meditation, I created the following guided meditation. I've used it many times to enhance my gratitude practice, and it has helped me tremendously whenever I needed help finding the blessings in my everyday life.

—————— GUIDED MEDITATION SCRIPT——————

This is a great meditation to do at the beginning or end of the day.

Turn off your phone and free yourself of interruptions.

Either sit or lie down, whatever is most comfortable, and close your eyes.

Take a long, slow, deep breath in, then slowly exhale.

Feel your tension melt away as you gradually relax deeper with each breath.

Take another long, slow, deep breath in, then exhale.

Feel yourself drift into a state of deep relaxation.

Continue to breathe slowly and gently as you bring your awareness to the top of your head.

Picture a warm, loving golden light spread from the top of your head down to your toes.

Feel your muscles relax as the light washes over you, surrounding and protecting you.

Take a few more deep breaths and relax deeply.

In this safe, relaxed state, reflect on all the things you're grateful for: loved ones, breath in your lungs, sunshine, fresh air, the tasty dinner you had that evening, a nice compliment from a coworker—whatever comes to mind.

As each object of gratitude appears, visualize yourself saying thank you to each thing.

Picture the person you're grateful for standing in front of you, and tell them how grateful you are for them and why.

Try to make the image and feeling as real as you can.

Taste the delicious apple you ate for lunch and say thank you to it.

If you're having a difficult time coming up with things to be grateful for, ask God, a Higher Power, or the highest part of yourself to reveal them to you.

Allow the feeling of deep gratitude to come into your body.

Notice where the feeling is in your body.

Take a few deep breaths and allow it to expand.

Enjoy the pleasant feeling gratitude gives you, and feel it wash away your tension and negativity.

You can remain in this relaxed state as long as you'd like.

When you're ready, end your gratitude meditation with the following affirmation:

"Thank you for the many blessings I have been bestowed with. May these blessings multiply as I continue to notice and give thanks for them. Thank you, Universe. Amen."

Wiggle your toes and fingers, open your eyes, and give yourself a few moments to adjust.

Bring that feeling of gratitude with you as you go through your day or drift off to sleep.

Full-Body Gratitude Meditation to Tame Negative Self-Talk and Love Yourself Just As You Are

What would happen if you loved your body unconditionally? Do you think it would change how you move through each day? The answer is absolutely yes.

When you can love your body unconditionally, you can love all things unconditionally. It's so easy to take our bodies for granted, but it's our reason for living. Give it the gratitude it deserves, and watch how loving your body just as it changes your entire life.

——— GUIDED MEDITATION SCRIPT ———

Close your eyes, and take a few calming breaths in through the nose and out through the mouth.

Take a few more deep, calming breaths and feel yourself relaxing with each exhale.

Visualize a beautiful, shimmery, green light gently coming into your body through your feet and up to the top of your head, bathing your entire body.

This beautiful green light washes away all your stress and tension and soothes your body.

The color green is said to be universally healing because it's symbolic for the heart chakra.

Visualizing the color green helps you tap into the frequency of unconditional love.

Let's tap into that beautiful, loving energy right now for your body.

Visualize the green light moving to your feet and toes.

Watch as your mind's eye shows you how much you use your feet each day to walk, stand, and move from place to place.

Feel your heart fill with gratitude for all your feet do for you, and say silently or out loud: "I love you, feet and toes. Thank you."

Now, feel the soft green light move up your legs and hips, and see in your mind's eye how much your legs and hips support your body.

Think of all the times you've used your legs and hips for movement and support. Feel gratitude come into your heart and say: "I love you, legs and hips. Thank you."

Watch the green light move into your stomach and visualize all the major organs that power your digestion, allowing you to enjoy and process everything you eat and drink.

Relish in how amazing it is that your intestines, liver, kidneys, gallbladder, and pancreas all work together to nourish your body and eliminate waste.

Feel gratitude for the incredible gift this part of your body provides by saying: "I love you, stomach and digestive system. Thank you."

Now, move the green light up to your chest and see all the organs that power your body, like your lungs and heart.

Visualize how your lungs and heart work every moment to keep you alive and breathing.

Send love and appreciation to this wondrous part of your body by saying: "I love you, chest, lungs, and heart. Thank you."

Move the green light into your arms and hands, and in your mind's eye, see how much you rely on them each day to touch and hold the things you need.

Feel gratitude fill your heart as you give thanks for them by saying, "I love you, arms and hands. Thank you."

Finally, move the green light up your neck and throat to your head.

Imagine all the gifts your throat and head provide, like eyes that can see, ears that can hear, a nose that can smell, a mouth that can taste, and a throat that can speak.

Feel the overwhelming gratitude you have for all these parts of your body and say: "I love you, throat, eyes, ears, nose, mouth, head, and neck. Thank you."

Now, feel the beautiful green light fill your entire body and bathe it in love.

The green light washes over every single part of your body and fills your heart with love and gratitude for every single cell.

Say: "I love you, body. Thank you."

Take a few moments to enjoy this feeling of unconditional love for your body.

When you're ready, open your eyes, wiggle your fingers and toes, and take this feeling with you as you move through the rest of your day.

Soulful Gratitude in Advance Meditation
to Bring Your Best Life into Being

Giving gratitude in advance is an extremely powerful way to set your intentions for the future. The law of attraction states that what you put into the world is what you will get out of it. Simply, what you think is what you create in your life.

If we think negative thoughts, we can attract negative situations. Likewise, if we live a life of gratitude, we will never run out of things to be grateful for. This powerful guided gratitude meditation will help you open your eyes and see the many blessings that have been given to you so you can lay the groundwork for even more gifts to come.

———— GUIDED MEDITATION SCRIPT ————

Find a comfortable place to sit, and close your eyes. Take a deep breath in, then exhale.

Relax your mind and body. Take another gentle breath in, then exhale.

Take a moment to review your life as it is right now. Think of all the people, places, and things you encounter each day. What are you most grateful for?

Allow yourself to feel gratitude for each of these things.

Let that deep feeling of gratitude enter your heart. Your life is perfect just as it is right now.

Take a few more slow, deep breaths and allow this feeling to expand.

Enjoy the pleasant feeling gratitude gives you, and feel it wash away your tension and negativity.

Now, call into your mind what you wish for your future.

Think about the next month, year, or longer. Visualize what you want to create in your life, be it loving relationships, a healthy body, greater abundance, a satisfying career, world peace—whatever brings you great joy.

Now, imagine your visualizations coming true.

Tune into the way you would feel if these dreams were fulfilled. Do you feel joyful, inspired, fulfilled, free?

Feel deep gratitude for each of your visualizations manifesting in your life.

Say thank you to each of these images, relishing in how good it feels to have your dreams manifest.

Now, visualize yourself letting go of the images and giving them to a Higher Power or the highest form of yourself.

Your dreams are in good hands, and they will be answered in divine time.

When you're ready, end your gratitude meditation with the following affirmation: "Thank you for the many blessings I have already been given and for the many blessings that are on their way to me now."

Open your eyes and give yourself a few moments to adjust.

You can write your dreams in a journal or notebook if you wish, then refer back to them as you see them come true.

In the days after doing this meditation, be on the lookout for any signs or insights that can lead you toward fulfilling your wishes.

Often, answers are presented through people, signs, books, or dreams.

Either way, when you feel like your dream is coming true, write it down, but most importantly, give gratitude for it when it does.

Five-Minutes Meditations for a Peaceful World

Send Out Positive Energy Meditation
to Bless Everyone in Your Life

Heal Mother Earth
in Love and Kindness Meditation

Send Out Positive Energy Meditation
to Bless Everyone in Your Life

Every day offers us the opportunity to appreciate the people in our lives who make the world a brighter place. In this meditation, you will take a few moments to send your blessings to these beautiful souls and watch them blossom.

You can also send blessings to those you do not know personally. The act of blessing someone else returns the blessing to you one-hundredfold.

Warning: This meditation can be habit-forming. You may suddenly find yourself blessing your boss, random strangers while you're driving, your dentist, and anyone else you encounter during the day. You won't believe how good it will make you feel.

——————— GUIDED MEDITATION SCRIPT ———————

Close your eyes, and take some relaxed breaths, which will allow you to get into a calm, peaceful state.

Nothing else needs to happen in this moment; simply focus on your breathing.

As you breathe, think of three people you would like to send your blessings to. It could be friends, family, service workers, or even strangers.

Bring the first person to mind, and see them filled with light and love. Say to them, "May you be blessed."

Bring the second person to mind and see them filled with light and love. Say, "May you be blessed."

Bring forth the last person, see them filled with light and love, and say, "May you be blessed."

Wonderful.

Now call to mind someone you are having challenges with.

Yes, we are sending out blessings to those who may cause us issues or challenges too.

Jesus said, "Bless your enemies" because it is a powerful form of healing not only for them, but for you as well.

See this person in your mind, filled with light and love.

Call on Jesus or any other Higher Power to help you with your blessing and say, "May you be blessed."

Is there anyone else you'd like to take a moment and share a blessing with? Is there anyone you feel overwhelmed with gratitude for?

Call them to mind now, filled with light and love, and say to them, "May you be blessed."

As you bring this meditation to a close, take in a long, deep breath to allow yourself to reconnect with the present.

You will finish the meditation by blessing yourself. There is nothing wrong with blessing yourself.

You cannot pour out to others from an empty cup, so making sure you send a blessing to yourself allows you to continue to give blessings to others.

Place your hands over your heart, see yourself filled with light and love, and say to yourself, "May you be blessed."

Open your eyes and continue to bless people as you carry on with your day.

Heal Mother Earth in Love and Kindness Meditation

Mother Earth is incredible, and we are beyond lucky to call Her our home. Our earth feeds, nourishes, provides, and gives so much for us. Why not give something back?

This is a beautiful mediation that allows you to share your love and gratitude with Earth and connect with nature on a deeper level. If you'd like, you can find a quiet spot outside to complete this meditation to enhance the experience even further.

——— GUIDED MEDITATION SCRIPT ———

Sit or lie in a comfortable position. If you are outside for this meditation, feel free to stand with your bare feet planted on the ground.

Begin by taking a few moments to breathe deeply.

Take a few long, deep breaths in through your nose and a long, gentle exhale out the mouth.

Don't rush this process, as it allows you to get into a calm, comfortable state of being.

It allows your mind to quiet and your body to relax naturally.

Close your eyes if they aren't already, and visualize Earth as you allow your breathing to return to a natural rhythm.

See the details of all Her waters, including oceans, lakes, rivers, and seas.

As you visualize these areas, see them pure, clear, and healthy, able to support all life that call them home.

See the fish, whales, dolphins, sea turtles, and coral basking and thriving in this beautiful clean water.

Visualize a golden light shining within your heart, and send this light to all the waters of Earth, blessing it.

Ask your Higher Power to direct your prayer to all the waters of the planet.

Next, see the land of our planet, including the soil, trees, and rainforests.

Picture the land purged of all toxicity and healed; see the dark richness of the soil and the lush green of the rainforests.

See all the animals of the land living in perfect harmony within it.

Once again, send the golden light within your heart to all the land of Earth, blessing it.

Ask your Higher Power to direct your prayer to the lands of the planet.

Now visualize Earth's atmosphere, Her blue skies, puffy clouds, and crystal clear air that surrounds our planet.

Picture yourself breathing in clean, pure air and see everyone around the world enjoying this crystal clean air too.

Watch as all the winged beings fly in the sky, enjoying the fresh and clean air.

Send the golden light shining within your heart to Earth's air and atmosphere, blessing it.

Ask your Higher Power to direct your prayer to the air and atmosphere of the planet.

Now, direct the loving, golden light of your heart to a healthy and harmonious world, and pray for your visions to become reality.

Take one more long, deep, cleansing breath as you reconnect with your surroundings.

Thank Mother Earth for all She has provided and for being our home.

Thank Her for the gorgeous sunrises that bring hope each morning.

Thank Her for the diamond-like stars that illuminate the darkest night, reminding us to reflect as we shine in this world.

Thank Mother Earth for bringing your life into being and continuing to love and support you each and every day.

When you are ready, open your eyes and return to your day feeling refreshed and excited to enjoy all that this world has to offer.

Namaste.

BIBLIOGRAPHY

Part I: How to Set Your Meditation Practice Up for Success

Lam, A. (2015, March 26) "Effects of Five-Minute Mindfulness Meditation on Mental Health Care Professionals," *Journal of Psychology & Clinical Psychiatry.* https://medcraveonline.com/JPCPY/effects-of-five-minute-mindfulness-meditation-on-mental-health-care-professionals.html.

Cronkleton, Emily. (2017, May 24) "Meditation Poses: In the Desk, On the Floor, and More," Healthline. https://www.healthline.com/health/mental-health/meditation-positions#sitting.

Part II: 30 Amazing Guided Meditations You Can Do in Just Five Minutes a Day

Brennan, Dan. (2021, June 9) "What to Know About 4-7-8 Breathing," *WebMD.* https://www.webmd.com/balance/what-to-know-4-7-8-breathing.

Capone, Mary and Janet Rupp. *The 5-Minute Healer.* Johnson Books, 2002.

Rahn, Flicka. "Healing Vocal Toning With Flicka Rahn," *Aristology.* https://www.crowdcast.io/e/vocal-toning-with-flicka/register.

Chakra Toning. *Sound Intentions.* https://www.soundintentions.com/sound-healing/exercises/chakra-toning.

Dwoskin, Hale. *The Sedona Method.* Sedona Press, 2003.

Anziani, Madhu. (2021, August 20) Activate Your Chakras By Chanting the Bija Mantras. *Yoga Journal.* https://www.yogajournal.com/live-be-yoga-featured/activate-chakras-with-bija-mantras.

Robinson, Josie. (2020, December 16) "The Amazing Secret to How Manifesting Really Works," *The Gratitude Jar.* https://josierobinson.com/journal/how-to-manifest.

Robinson, Josie. (2019, July 19) "5 Simple Self-Love Exercises That Will Heal Your Life," *The Gratitude Jar.* https://josierobinson.com/journal/self-compassion-practices.

Robinson, Josie. *Give Thanks.* Wise Ink Creative Publishing, 2018.

ABOUT THE AUTHOR

JOSIE ROBINSON is a bestselling author who helps every-day people navigate this chaotic modern world with gratitude and grace. She believes anyone can learn to find peace in the present moment, no matter what the present moment may bring. Josie lives in Minnesota with her husband, sons, and a chatty black cat.

Made in the USA
Las Vegas, NV
02 January 2023

64500897R00076